WORD PROBLEMS
USING
RATIOS
AND
PROPORTIONS

MASTERING MATH WORD PROBLEMS

Zella Williams and
Rebecca Wingard-Nelson

Enslow Publishing
101 W. 23rd Street
Suite 240
New York, NY 10011
USA

enslow.com

Published in 2017 by Enslow Publishing, LLC.
101 W. 23rd Street, Suite 240, New York, NY 10011

Library of Congress Cataloging-in-Publication Data

Names: Williams, Zella, author. | Wingard-Nelson, Rebecca, author.
Title: Word problems using ratios and proportions / Zella Williams and
  Rebecca Wingard-Nelson.
Description: New York, NY : Enslow Publishing, 2017. | Series: Mastering math
  word problems | Includes bibliographical references and index.
Identifiers: LCCN 2016032318| ISBN 9780766082748 (library bound) | ISBN
  9780766082724 (pbk.) | ISBN 9780766082731 (6 pack)
Subjects: LCSH: Ratio and proportion—Juvenile literature. | Word problems
  (Mathematics)—Juvenile literature. | Problem solving—Juvenile literature.
Classification: LCC QA117 .W5678 2017 | DDC 513.2/4—dc23
LC record available at https://lccn.loc.gov/2016032318

Printed in China

To Our Readers: We have done our best to make sure all websites in this book were active and appropriate when we went to press. However, the author and the publisher have no control over and assume no liability for the material available on those websites or on any websites they may link to. Any comments or suggestions can be sent by email to customerservice@enslow.com.

Portions of this book originally appeared in the book *Space Word Problems Starring Ratios and Proportions*.

Photo Credits: Cover, p. 1 © iStockphoto.com/Christopher Futcher; pp. 3, 14 BSIP/UIG/Getty Images; p. 4 Monkey Business Images/Thinkstock; p. 7 NASA/Getty Images; p. 8 Mopic/Shutterstock.com; pp. 9, 11 Hugh Threlfall/Photolibrary/Getty Images; p. 12 martin_adams2000/iStock/Thinkstock; p. 16 wnjay_wootthisak/iStock/Thinkstock; p. 18 Sovfoto/Universal Images Group/Getty Images; p. 21 Aaron MCcoy/Photolibrary/Getty Images; p. 23 3DSculptor/iStock/Thinkstock; p. 25 MarcelC/iStock/Thinkstock; p. 27 Tristan3D/Shutterstock.com; p. 29 Stockbyte/Thinkstock; p. 30 m-gucci/iStock/Thinkstock; p. 33 Digital Vision/Photodisc/Thinkstock; p. 35 ChrisGorgio/iStock/Thinkstock; p. 37 Brady Barrineau/Shutterstock.com; p. 39 Nikada/E+/Getty Images; p. 43 sdecoret/Shutterstock.com; p. 47 bluelela/Shutterstock.com; cover and interior pages icons and graphics Shutterstock.com: Anna_leni (owl), Draze Design (pad and pencil), RedlineVector (light bulb), Yuri Gayvoronskiy (eyes), james Weston (scrambled numbers), Ratoca (thumbs up).

Contents

Homework problems are your practice for solving word problems.

Word Problems: Problem Solved!

 ## Tips for Solving Word Problems

Word problems might come up in your homework, on a test, or even in your life. These tips can help you solve them, no matter where they show up.

 ## Be positive!

It's great when you get a problem right the first time. It's even better when you don't get a problem right the first time, but you learn from your mistakes! You learned something new!

 ## Get help early!

Don't be afraid to ask for help. New problems build on old ones. If you don't understand today's problem, get help so tomorrow's problem is easier to understand.

 ## Do your homework!

The more you practice something, the better you become at it. You don't expect to play an instrument or a sport perfectly the first time you do it, right? Of course not! Learning new things takes practice.

 Move on!

If you get stuck, move on to the next problem. Do the problems you know how to solve first. That way, you won't miss the ones you know because you ran out of time. Go back later and try the problems you skipped.

Ask questions!

When someone is helping you, asking questions tells the person what you don't understand. If you don't ask questions, you will never get answers!

Take a break!

If you have tried everything you can think of but are only getting frustrated, take a break. Close your eyes and take a deep breath. Stretch your arms and legs. Get a drink of water or a snack. Then come back and try again.

Don't give up!

The first time you try to solve a word problem, you might come up with an answer that does not make sense. Don't give up! Check your math. Try solving the problem a different way. If you quit, you won't learn.

Ratios and Proportions

Ratios compare numbers. For example, there were 35 astronauts selected to enter NASA's space program in 1978. Of these, 6 were female and 29 were male.

This is the 2007 space shuttle crew. There were two women and five men on this flight.

Ratios can compare two parts of something, such as female to male astronauts (6 to 29), or a part and a whole, such as female astronauts to all astronauts (6 to 35). Ratios can even compare related, but different, things, such as a number of astronauts and how much food they eat each day.

Ratios can be written in three ways:

Using the word "to"	Using a colon	Using a fraction bar
6 to 29	6 : 29	29/6

The numbers in a ratio are called terms. In the ratio 6 : 29, the first term is 6, and the second term is 29.

Proportions compare two ratios.

On Mars, you weigh only 1 pound for every 3 pounds you weigh on Earth. That means if you weigh 50 pounds on Mars, you weigh 150 pounds on Earth.

Mars is the fourth planet from the sun. It is the second smallest planet in the solar system.

A proportion uses the equal sign to show that two ratios have the same value.

3 pounds = 150 pounds

1 pound = 50 pounds

Rates are special ratios.

The average cost of a space shuttle mission is $450 million.

Rates use the word "per" or a fraction bar to compare numbers with different units, like dollars and missions. Some other examples of rates are "dollars per pound" and "miles per hour."

The cost of a space shuttle mission is $450 million per mission, or $450 million/mission.

Solving Problems Using Ratios and Proportions

❗ Take It Step by Step

Word problems can be solved by following four easy steps.

❓ Here's the problem.

A five-day spaceflight is being planned. Each astronaut can pick two snacks per day. At this rate, how many snacks can each astronaut choose for the entire flight?

Food for space flights is often freeze dried, like this astronaut ice cream. Freeze-dried food lasts a very long time and is easy to store.

Step 1 Read and understand the problem.

Read the problem carefully.

Ask yourself questions, like:

What do you know?

The spaceflight is five days long.

Each astronaut can choose 2 snacks per day.

What are you trying to find?

How many snacks each astronaut can choose.

What kind of problem is this?

This is a rate problem. The rate is two snacks per day. This rate problem gives you the rate of snacks for one day and wants you to find the number of snacks for five days.

It is a multiplication problem.

Step 2 Make a plan.

Some problems tell you how they should be solved. They may say "draw a picture" or "make a table." For other problems, you need to make your own plan. Use whatever plan makes the most sense and is easiest for you. Some plans you might try are:

Look for a pattern	Write an equation
Estimate	Use a model
Guess and check	Break it apart
Make a list	Use a table
Make a drawing	Use logical reasoning

How can you solve this problem?

You can write a multiplication equation.

Step 3 Solve the problem.

It is time to do the math!

If you find that your plan is not working, make a new plan. Don't give up the first time. Write your answer. Make sure you include the units.

Let's write the equation.

Multiply the number of days by the number of snacks per day.

$$\begin{array}{r} 5 \text{ days} \\ \times 2 \text{ snacks per day} \\ \hline 10 \text{ snacks} \end{array}$$

Each astronaut can choose 10 snacks.

Step 4 Look back.

The problem is solved! But you aren't finished yet. Take a good look at your answer. **Does it make sense? Did you use the right numbers to begin?** Estimate or use the inverse operation to check your math.

Did you include the units in your answer?

Yes.

Could you have solved the problem another way?

Yes. You could draw a picture to show two snacks each day for five days. Then count the total number of snacks.

| **Day 1** | **Day 2** | **Day 3** | **Day 4** | **Day 5** |

There are 10 snacks in all.

Read a Table

Sometimes you need to use information from a table to solve a problem.

 ## Here's the problem.

There are eight planets in our solar system. Some of the planets are made of rock. Others are made of gas. Use the table to find the ratio of the planets made of rock to the total planets in our solar system.

Jupiter is the fifth planet from the sun and the largest in our solar system. It is made up mainly of gas.

Planet Name	Gas	Rock
Earth		X
Jupiter	X	
Mars		X
Mercury		X
Neptune	X	
Saturn	X	
Uranus	X	
Venus		X

Read and understand.

What do you know?

The planets in our solar system are made of rock or gas.

What are you trying to find?

The ratio of planets made of rock to total planets in our solar system.

Plan.

Use the table to find the number of planets that are made of rock. Then write a ratio.

Solve.

This ratio compares the number of planets made of rock to the total number of planets in our solar system. Use the table to count the number of planets that are made of rock.

Four planets—Earth, Mars, Mercury, and Venus— are made of rock.

The problem tells you there are eight planets in our solar system.

For our solar system, the ratio of planets made of rock to total planets is 4 to 8.

Look back.

Did you answer the right question?

Yes.

Could you have answered in a different way?

Yes. Ratios can be written using a colon, 4:8, or using a fraction bar, 4/8.

! Comparison Sentences

A ratio in fraction form can be used in a comparison sentence.

? Here's the problem.

The distance from Earth to the sun is called an astronomical unit (AU). Neptune is 30 AUs from the sun. Write a sentence using the words "as far as" to compare the distances from Neptune and Earth to the sun.

Earth is the third planet from the sun, while Neptune is the farthest planet from the sun.

Read and understand.

What do you know?

Earth is 1 AU from the sun.

Neptune is 30 AUs from the sun.

What are you trying to find?

A sentence that uses "as far as" to compare the distances from Earth and Neptune to the sun.

Plan.

A ratio can be written as a fraction. The fraction can be used in a sentence to compare the two distances. Let's write a ratio as a fraction, then write a sentence.

Solve.

Write the ratio.

Distance in AUs from Earth to the sun: 1

Distance in AUs from Neptune to the sun: 30

So the ratio is 1:30 or 1/30.

Now write a sentence.

Earth is 1/30 as far as Neptune from the sun.

Look back.

What happens if you put the terms in a different order (Neptune first)?

The ratio becomes 30/1, so the sentence is:

Neptune is 30 times as far as Earth from the sun.

Logical Reasoning

Although ratios can be written in fraction form, they are not fractions.

Here's the problem.

Stars are labeled with a letter based on their type. The seven main types of stars are O, B, A, F, G, K, and M. Types O and B are very bright but uncommon. M stars are common but not very bright.

On Monday night, Kory saw 2 B stars and 28 M stars. On Tuesday night, he saw 1 B star and 30 M stars. Give the ratio of B stars to M stars for Monday night, Tuesday night, and the two nights combined.

The sun is the closest star to Earth, but we can see thousands of stars in the night sky. They seem small, but many of those tiny lights come from stars hundreds of times larger than the sun!

Read and understand.

What do you know?

On Monday night, Kory saw 2 B stars and 28 M stars.

On Tuesday night, Kory saw 1 B star and 30 M stars.

What are you trying to find?

Three ratios:

B to M stars on Monday night,

B to M stars on Tuesday night, and

B to M stars on the two nights together.

Plan.

Let's write the ratios for Monday and Tuesday night, then add to find the ratio for the two nights together.

Solve.

Monday night: Tuesday night:

	Monday night	Tuesday night
B stars	2	1
M stars	28	30

The ratio of B to M starts is 2 to 28 and 1 to 30.

Ratios are NOT added or subtracted in the same way as fractions. To find the third ratio, decide how you can find the ratio for the two nights combined. You must find the total number of B stars for both nights, and the total number of M stars for both nights.

Monday B stars + Tuesday B stars $2 + 1 = 3$

Monday M stars + Tuesday M stars $28 + 30 = 58$

The ratio of B stars to M stars for Monday night is 2 to 28. For Tuesday night it is 1 to 30. For the two nights combined it is 3 to 58.

 Look back.

Did you answer all three questions?
Yes.

Did you start with the right numbers?
Yes.

 Equivalent Ratios

Ratios that have the same value, such as 1 to 3 and 2 to 6, are called equivalent.

 Here's the problem.

A dog that weighs 12 pounds on Earth would weigh only 2 pounds on the moon. Using the same ratio, how much would a person who weighs 120 pounds on Earth weigh on the moon?

In 1957, Laika was the first dog to travel into space. She rode in a Russian space capsule called *Sputnik 2.*

Read and understand.

What do you know?

A dog that weighs 12 pounds on Earth would weigh 2 pounds on the moon.

What are you trying to find?

How much a person who weighs 120 pounds on Earth would weigh on the moon.

Plan.

The problem says "using the same ratio." Let's find the ratio of the dog's weight on Earth and weight on the moon first, then change it to match the person's weight on Earth.

Solve.

Find the ratio.

DOG:

Earth weight   12 pounds

Moon weight   2 pounds

Change the ratio to higher terms by multiplying each term by the same number. The person weighs 120 pounds on Earth. To change Earth weight (12) to 120, you multiply by 10. Multiply each term by 10.

PERSON:

Earth weight   12 pounds $\times$ 10 = 120 pounds

Moon weight   2 pounds $\times$ 10 = 20 pounds

The person who weighs 120 pounds on Earth would weigh 20 pounds on the moon.

Look back.

Does your answer make sense?
Yes.

Why?
Because the person weighs 10 times as much as the dog on Earth, and 10 times as much as the dog on the moon.

Ways to Solve Word Problems

❗ Use Mental Math

When the numbers in a problem are easy to work with, you can use mental math.

❓ Here's the problem.

One night Charla saw 40 flying objects, but she could not identify 2. Write the ratio of the unidentified flying objects to the total number of flying objects she saw. Write the ratio in lowest terms.

When Venus is bright, hundreds of people report that they see a UFO. Often, UFO sightings are just ordinary objects in the sky.

Read and understand.

What do you know?

Charla saw 40 flying objects.

She could not identify 2 of the flying objects.

What are you trying to find?

The ratio in lowest terms of flying objects she could not identify to flying objects she saw.

What is lowest terms?

When the ratio cannot be reduced any lower.

Plan.

Let's write the ratio, then reduce it to lowest terms.

Solve.

Write the ratio.

flying objects not identified	:	flying objects in all
2	:	40

Remember, you can multiply or divide each term of a ratio by the same number without changing the value of the ratio.

Both 2 and 40 can be divided by 2 in your head.

2 ÷ 2	:	40 ÷ 2
1	:	20

The ratio of flying objects Charla could not identify to flying objects she saw is 1:20.

Look back.

Check the math. Use multiplication to check division.
Multiply each term (1 and 20) by the number you divided by (2).
If the products are the numbers you started with, then your math is correct.

Did you start with 2 and 40?
Yes.

$1 \times 2 = 2$
$20 \times 2 = 40$

Use Paper and Pencil

When numbers are too hard to use in your head, you can use a paper and pencil to do the math.

Here's the problem.

A rocket uses 105 kilograms of fuel in 30 seconds. Write a rate to show how fast the fuel is used by the rocket. Make sure the rate is in lowest terms.

Carrier rockets bring a payload, such as a satellite, into space.

Read and understand.

What do you know?

The rocket uses 105 kilograms of fuel in 30 seconds.

What are you trying to find?

The rate at which the rocket uses fuel.

What is a rate?

A rate is a ratio that uses the word "per" or a fraction bar to compare numbers with different units. Some examples of rates are "dollars per pound" and "miles per hour."

Plan.

Let's write a ratio that is a rate, then reduce it to lowest terms.

Solve.

Write the rate.

Amount of fuel used: 105 kilograms

Time: 30 seconds

So the rate is 105 kg per 30 seconds.

Reduce the rate to lowest terms. You can divide more than one time to get to lowest terms.

If you cannot divide the numbers in your head, use a paper and pencil.

$105 \text{ kg} \div 5 = 21 \text{ kg} \div 3 = 7 \text{ kg}$

$30 \text{ s} \div 5 = 6 \text{ s} \div 3 = 2 \text{ s}$

The rocket uses fuel at a rate of 7 kilograms per 2 seconds.

 Look back.

Is there something you could have done differently?

Yes. To reduce the rate to lowest terms, divide 105 and 30 by their greatest common factor, 15.

$105 \text{ kg} \div 15 = 7 \text{ kg}$

$30 \text{ s} \div 15 = 2 \text{ s}$

This way you only need to divide once!

 # Use a Calculator

When you need an accurate answer fast, or the numbers are too hard to calculate by hand, you can use a calculator.

 Here's the problem.

It took a flash of light on the moon 1.34 seconds to be seen on Earth. The moon was 401,721 kilometers from Earth. Write a unit rate to the nearest kilometer for the speed of the light.

The moon is one of the largest natural satellites in our solar system. It takes about 27 days for the moon to orbit Earth.

Read and understand.

What do you know?

From Earth, it took 1.34 seconds to see a light from the moon.

The moon was 401,721 kilometers from Earth.

What are you trying to find?

A unit rate for the speed of the light.

What is a unit rate?

A unit rate is a rate with one unit as the second term. Unit rates are usually written without the 1, such as 5 miles per hour instead of 5 miles per 1 hour.

What is speed?

Speed is a rate that compares distance to time.

Plan.

Write the rate for the speed.

Reduce the rate so that 1 is the second term.

Solve.

Write the rate for speed.

Distance: 401,721 km

Time: 1.34 s

To find any unit rate, you can divide each term by the second term. 401,721 ÷ 1.34 is a hard problem, so use a calculator. Round the answer to the nearest whole number.

$401,721 \text{ km} \div 1.34 = 299,792 \text{ km}$

$1.34 \text{ s} \div 1.34 = 1 \text{ s}$

The speed of the light is 299,792 km per second.

 Look back.

When is a good time to use a calculator?

1. When the problem is hard and your teacher says that you can.
2. To check your answers.
3. When you need a fast, accurate answer.

 # Multiplying Rates

Problems that give you a rate are often multiplication or division problems.

 ## Here's the problem.

Neptune spins at a rate of 16 hours per rotation. How many hours does Neptune take to rotate five times?

Neptune is the farthest known planet from the sun in our solar system. It takes Neptune 165 years to orbit the sun.

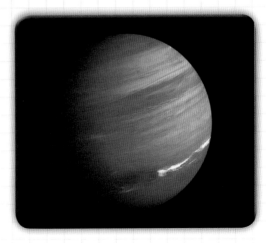

Read and understand.

What do you know?

Neptune spins at 16 hours per rotation.

What are you trying to find?

How many hours Neptune takes to rotate five times.

Plan.

Sixteen hours per rotation is a unit rate.

It means one rotation takes 16 hours.

To find how many hours five rotations take, you can multiply. Let's write an equation.

Solve.

Multiply the number of hours one rotation takes (16) by the number of rotations (5).

$$\begin{array}{r} 16 \\ \times\,5 \\ \hline 80 \end{array}$$

It takes Neptune 80 hours to rotate five times.

Look back.

Does the answer make sense?

Yes.

Is there another way you can solve this problem?

Yes. You could add the time it takes for one rotation (16 hours) five times.

$16 + 16 + 16 + 16 + 16 = 80$

Use a Formula

A formula is an equation that shows how quantities and rates are related.

Here's the problem.

A rocket traveled at a rate of 25,000 miles per hour for three hours. How many miles did it travel? Use the formula *distance = speed × time*, or *d = st*.

To orbit Earth, a space shuttle travels at about 17,500 miles per hour. To escape Earth's gravity, a rocket must travel at least 25,000 miles per hour.

Read and understand.

What do you know?

The rocket speed was 25,000 miles per hour.
The rocket traveled for three hours.

What are you trying to find?

The number of miles the rocket traveled.

Plan.

The problem gives you a formula to find distance. Let's use the formula.

Solve.

Write the formula.

distance = speed × time

Put the numbers you know in the formula.

distance = 25,000 mph × 3 h

25,000 × 3 = 75,000

The rocket traveled 75,000 miles.

Look back.

Why is the answer in miles?

Because the speed was given in miles per hour, and the problem asked for a number of miles.

Change Units

Units in a rate can be changed in the same way you convert units that are not in a rate.

Here's the problem.

The speed of light is about 300,000 kilometers per second. What is the speed of light in kilometers per hour?

The Andromeda Galaxy is a spiral galaxy that is about 2.5 million light-years from Earth.

Read and understand.

What do you know?

The speed of light is 300,000 kilometers per second.

What are you trying to find?

A rate in kilometers per hour that is the same as 300,000 kilometers per second.

Plan.

Let's convert seconds to minutes, then minutes to hours.

Solve.

The original rate is 300,000 kilometers per second, or per 1 second.

There are 60 seconds in one minute. Multiply BOTH the distance (300,000 kilometers) AND the number of seconds (1) by 60.

300,000 kilometers × 60 = 18,000,000 kilometers
1 second × 60 = 60 seconds (1 minute)

Now do the same thing again. There are 60 minutes in one hour. Multiply BOTH the distance AND the number of minutes (1) by 60.

18,000,000 km × 60 = 1,080,000,000 km

1 minute × 60 = 60 minutes (1 hour)

300,000 kilometers per second is the same speed as 1,080,000,000 kilometers per hour.

 Look back.

Is there another way you can solve this problem?
Yes. If you know there are 3,600 seconds in one hour, you can multiply in one step instead of two.

Other Ways to Solve Problems

! Use a Model

Models can help you understand and solve some problems.

? Here's the problem.

A teacher splits her class into groups to study Saturn and its rings. They have models in a ratio of 4 cardboard rings for every one cardboard Saturn. If they use 25 cardboard pieces in all, how many groups are there if each group gets one Saturn?

Saturn is known for its many rings. It has nine main rings and three arcs made up of ice and other matter. It also has 62 moons in orbit around it.

Read and understand.

What do you know?

The ratio of cardboard rings to Saturns is 4 to 1.

33

The class is split into groups with one Saturn each. The class uses 25 cardboard pieces in all.

What are you trying to find?

The number of groups in the class.

Plan.

Let's use a model. You can use anything as a model. Beans, counters, chips, pennies, or cereal will work for this problem. Let's use beans.

Solve.

You know that 25 pieces are used in all, so start with 25 beans.

Make a group with one bean for the Saturn piece, and four beans for the ring pieces.

Keep making groups until you run out of beans.

Count the groups. There are five.

The class is split into five groups.

Look back.

Check your answer.

You know each group gets one Saturn piece and four ring pieces, or five total pieces.

5 pieces for each group $\times$ 5 groups = 25 pieces

! Write a Proportion

A proportion uses an equal sign to show that ratios are equal.

Here's the problem.

Mercury takes about 90 days to orbit the sun. Venus takes about 225 days. Is 2 to 3 the correct ratio for the time it takes Mercury to orbit the sun to the time it takes Venus to orbit the sun?

This picture of our solar system shows the orbits of each planet around the sun. Can you find Mercury and Venus here?

Read and understand.

What do you know?

Mercury takes 90 days to orbit the sun. Venus takes 225 days to orbit the sun.

What are you trying to find?

If the ratio of orbit times for Mercury and Venus is 2 to 3.

Plan.

A proportion is an equation with a ratio on each side. Let's write a proportion, and see if it is true.

Solve.

Write the proportion by putting an equal sign between what you know and what you read.

What you know:		What you read:
Mercury orbit time	90 days	2
Venus orbit time	225 days	3

Are the ratios equivalent? Reduce each ratio to lowest terms to check. You may need to reduce more than one time to get to lowest terms.

$$90 \div 5 = 18$$
$$18 \div 9 = \ \ 2$$
$$225 \div 5 = 45$$
$$45 \div 9 = \ \ 5$$

Does 2: 5 equal 2: 3?

No! The ratio of times for Mercury and Venus to orbit the sun is not 2 to 3.

Look back.

Did you start with the right numbers?
Yes.

Scale Drawings

A scale drawing is a picture that shows objects reduced or enlarged according to a proportion.

Here's the problem.

The diameter of Mars is about 7,000 kilometers. Saturn's diameter is about 120,000 kilometers. Kyle made a scale drawing of the solar system. His drawing of Mars has a diameter of 7 millimeters. What should the diameter of his drawing of Saturn be?

Mars is the second smallest planet in the solar system. It is only larger than Mercury. It is called the "Red Planet" because of its color.

Read and understand.

What do you know?

The diameter of Mars is about 7,000 km.

The diameter of Saturn is about 120,000 km.

The drawing of Mars has a diameter of 7 mm.

What are you trying to find?

What the diameter of Kyle's drawing of Saturn should be.

Plan.

Let's set up a proportion to find the missing diameter.

Solve.

	planet diameter	model diameter
Mars	7,000 km	7 mm
Saturn	120,000 km	?

You can divide 7,000 by 1,000 to get 7.

Divide 120,000 by 1,000 to find the missing term.

120,000 ÷ 1,000 = 120

	planet diameter	model diameter
Mars	7,000 km	7 mm
Saturn	120,000 km	120 mm

Kyle's drawing of Saturn should have a diameter of
120 millimeters.

Look back.

***The units of the real planets are in kilometers, but the
units in the model are in millimeters. Does that make
a difference?***

No. The ratios are still the same.

Cross Multiply

You can multiply the diagonal numbers in a proportion to see if the ratios have the same value.

Here's the problem.

For every seven parts of Earth's surface that are covered by water, there are three parts covered by land. Haven is making a globe using paper squares. She has 21 blue squares for the water, and 9 green squares for the land. Are the squares in the correct ratio?

Globes use ratios to make sure the continents and oceans are to scale. Earth is actually about 70 percent water and 30 percent land.

Read and understand.

What do you know?
The ratio of water to land on Earth's surface is 7 to 3.

What are you trying to find?
If the number of blue squares (21) to green squares (9) is in the same ratio as the water to land.

Plan.

Let's set up a proportion and check it.

Solve.

	Earth's surface		paper squares	
water	7	**=**	21	(blue)
land	3		9	(green)

To check if the ratios are the same, you can cross multiply. Multiply the numbers that are diagonal to each other in the proportion.

$7 \times 9 =$	63
$21 \times 3 =$	63

The products are the same, so the ratios are equal.

Haven has the correct ratio of blue to green paper squares.

Look back.

Is there another way you can check to see if the ratios are equal?

Yes. Reduce each ratio to lowest terms. You can divide both numbers by 3, which will give you the lowest terms.

$21 \div 3$	$= 7$
$9 \div 3$	$= 3$

Are the ratios equal?

Yes.

Scale Models

Scale models are in proportion to what they are modeling.

Here's the problem.

In a scale model of the solar system, Mercury is 2 inches from the sun and Pluto is 204 inches from the sun. The actual distance from Pluto to the sun is 3,672 million miles. How many millions of miles is Mercury from the sun?

Read and understand.

What do you know?

In the scale model, Mercury is 2 inches and Pluto is 204 inches from the sun. Pluto is 3,672 million miles from the sun.

What are you trying to find?

How far Mercury is from the sun.

Plan.

Let's set up a proportion.

Solve.

	scale distance from sun (inches)	actual distance from sun (millions of miles)
Mercury	2 in	?
Pluto	204 in	3,672

The cross products in a proportion are equal.

2 × 3,672 = 7,344
204 × ? = 7,344

Use division to find the missing number in the multiplication problem 204 × ? = 7,344.

7,344 ÷ 204 = 36

Mercury is 36 million miles from the sun.

Look back.

Did you start with the right numbers?

Yes. Use multiplication to check your division.

204 × 36 = 7,344

Estimation

You can use estimation when you do not need to know the exact answer to a problem.

Most meteorites are gray and hard. A few are black and fragile. In one area, 9,146 meteorites were found. If 3 of every 1,000 meteorites found are the black fragile type, about how many of those found are the black fragile type?

Meteorites are pieces of dust or rock from space that strike Earth's surface.

Read and understand.

What do you know?

There are 9,146 meteorites found. Three of every 1,000 meteorites found are the black fragile type.

What are you trying to find?

The number of black fragile meteorites that are found.

Is there anything special about this problem?

Yes. The problem asks "about how many."
The answer does not need to be exact.

Plan.

Let's estimate the answer by rounding 9,146 to the greatest place value, then setting up a proportion.

Solve.

Round 9,146 to the thousands place.

9,146 rounds to 9,000.

Set up the proportion.

Black, fragile	3	?
Total	1,000	9,000

1,000 multiplied by 9 is 9,000.

Multiply 3 × 9 to find the missing term.

3 × 9 = 27

Black, fragile	3	27
Total	1,000	9,000

About 27 of the 9,146 meteorites are the black, fragile type.

Look back.

Cross multiply to check your answer.

1,000 × 27 = 27,000
3 × 9,000 = 27,000

Remember the Plan

To solve a word problem, follow these steps:

Read and understand the problem.

Know what the problem says and what you need to find. If you don't understand, ask questions before you start.

Make a plan.

Choose the plan that makes the most sense and is easiest for you. Remember, there is usually more than one way to find the right answer.

Solve the problem.

Use the plan. If your first plan isn't working, try a different one. Take a break and come back with a fresh mind.

Look back.

Read the problem again. Make sure your answer makes sense. Check your math. If the answer does not look right, don't give up now! Use what you've learned to go back and try the problem again.

Glossary

calculator A tool used to solve math problems.

comparison The act of looking at two different equations or situations to show different levels of quality, quantity, or relation.

equations Number sentences that have two expressions that are equal in value on either side of the equals sign.

equivalent Equal in value.

estimation A rough calculation of the number, quantity, or value of something.

formula A mathematical relationship or rule that is expressed in numbers and symbols.

logical reasoning The process of using a rational, systematic series of steps based on sound mathematical procedures and given statements to arrive at a conclusion.

model A smaller copy of a person, structure, or thing.

proportion A set relationship between the quantity, size, shape, or position of two quantities.

ratio The relation between two amounts showing the number of times one value contains or is contained within the other.

scale The proportion or ratio that a drawing or model of an object bears to the object itself.

unit Whatever object that is being added or subtracted, such as the number of rings around a planet.

For More Information

Books

Clemson, David, and Wendy Clemson. *Rocket to the Moon.* Strongsville, OH: Gareth Stevens Publishing, 2007.

McCallum, Ann. *Rabbits Rabbits Everywhere: A Fibonacci Tale.* Watertown, MA: Charlesbridge Publishing, 2007.

Walsh, Kieran. *Space Math.* Vero Beach, FL: Rourke Publishing, 2006.

Websites

Aplusmath
www.aplusmath.com

Interactive math resources for teachers, parents, and students featuring free math worksheets, math games, math flashcards, and more.

Coolmath Games
www.coolmath-games.com

Try your hand at games that make learning and practicing math fun.

NASA
www.nasa.gov/audience/forstudents/index.html

Learn about space and astronauts through videos, photos, and games.

Index